I0470633

-Testimonials-
What "The Financial Plan..." has done for everyday people:

"Before, I never had money and was stressed because I never had enough for my expenses. I often had to go without *necessities* because I didn't have the money to purchase them. This book has helped me to realize unnecessary expenses and eliminate them. It has helped me to save, and now I have extra money."

-M.J. Harris
(mother on disability; current college student)

"I've learned money = management = opportunities. "The Financial Plan for Tip-Makers and Everyday People" has allowed me to see my money both in small or large amounts as a way to obtain anything... the smallest amounts are just as valuable as the larger ones. As a result, I used this plan to save $10,000 for the purchase of my first car!"

-Shanel Reeves
(former waitress; current retail store manager)

These are real quotes from people who *volunteered* to share their story. I assure you this is not a gimmick or a get rich quick scheme. It will take a little work and a little discipline, but you can gain control of your finances.

-Cornelious Jordan
(author)

THE FINANCIAL PLAN FOR TIP-MAKERS

AND

EVERYDAY PEOPLE

By Cornelious Jordan

TABLE OF CONTENTS

****
Where is my money going?

Hello, to all of my fellow tip makers out there! Bartenders, bussers, runners, barbers, and etc, I am a waiter and I wait tables. Greetings, to the people who work on fixed incomes such as hourly wage or salary, which I call "everyday people." If you don't relate to some of the things I mention about waiting tables, do not fret this financial plan is for you as well. I, at this time, am a waiter and have been for going on four years now. It's funny because the moment I typed the word "hello" a huge smile came over my face when I thought about waiting tables. I'm not smiling at the thought of customer service, mostly. I smile when I think about the staff and my fellow co-workers. We are kind of a family, aren't we? Everyday it's us against THEM: the lunch rush, the dinner crowd, the elderly couple who can't make up their minds, the screaming kids, and the teenagers who don't tip well. I also smile when I think of the various types of waiters. You have the "super bubbly" waiter whose voice gets really high when they approach a table, the "my life sucks" waiter who thinks they are smarter than everyone and often refers to people as stupid, the "everybody's friend" waiter who comes to work every Saturday morning smelling like alcohol, and "the flirt" ' nuff said. No matter what kind of waiter you are, all of us have a table that plum gets on our motherfreakin' nerves! As soon as we can get to the back room to refill their Diet Coke for the hundredth time or take that medium-well burger back to the kitchen, that they actually ordered medium-well, we are going to talk about them like a dog. After venting to our nearest co-worker, we gather ourselves together, put on that golden smile, and give the guest what they asked for. When the rush crowd has ended and the dust settles, we prop our feet on a nearby bar stool, and do what reminds us why we are waiters in the first place. We count that huge knot of cash in our pocket! There must be something about crazy tables, helping each other out, and a blind/deaf management team, because the first thing we do with that knot is what? Go to the local bar! And that's where the problems start.

Don't get me wrong, a night of drinks after work is awesome...Good times! Nevertheless, I can't tell you how many times I've gone home after a work shift and thought to myself, "What the heck happened to my money?" All of my co-workers, as I have, have often asked themselves the same question. We've joked about it, shrugged our shoulders, and did the same thing all over again. Anyone who's in the restaurant business knows there is a pattern. In the beginning of the month no one wants to really help out and pick up available shifts and servers are calling in one after the other trying to get their shifts covered because they want the day off. However, at the end of the month you can't seem to pick up a shift to save your life because everybody wants to keep their shift. If you need the day off, at the end of the month it's the best time. That's when waiters are like hounds and scrambling to pick up the next available shift. Why? The rent is due, that's why. All of that drinking, partying, and etc. has kicked you in the butt and bills are due on the 1st. We tip makers scramble at the end of the month because we know if we pick up enough shifts we can make up for all that goofing off, just like that. That's the best part about working for tips. The day you work is the day you get paid. How cool is it to get paid every time you go to work and still have a paycheck every two weeks, it's only a couple hundred dollars, but it's still a check. The worst part about working for tips is you take for granted that you make money daily, and you say to yourself, "Oh I'll make up for it the next time I work." When you delay and delay your expenses, that's what leaves you frantically trying to pick up shifts at the end of the month. I don't know about you, but with this recession the whole struggling at the end of the month thing become monotonous. Especially since people aren't going out to eat like they used to, as a result tips are low, and trying to pick up extra shifts isn't as easy as it used to be.

One day I was talking to one of my co-workers, and he was complaining about getting overdraft charges from his bank at the end of the month when he paid his rent. I was thinking, "You too?" That let me know right there, not only is he working from check to check, but he's not saving any money because as soon as he pays his rent it wipes him out. He also was not doing a good job of taking care of his expenses because everytime he paid his rent his account would go negative. I too was having the same problem. Now "everyday people" I know you are not tip makers, but does any of this sound familiar? Are you barely making ends meet? I think we can all relate to living check to check. So after three years of waiting tables I said to myself, "I need to do something about my financial situation and nothing was going to stop me." Now I'm not saying I haven't tried in the past. I've tried several ways to make large sums of money quickly. Shoot, that was the reason I started serving in the first place, it's fast money. So my wheels are turning. I try to budget my money better, I try picking up shifts at the beginning of the month instead of the end because it's easier, but I still was not making ends meet. One day I am watching our president Barack Obama give a speech. He was talking about our economic crisis and the war in Iraq. He said something like, "No nation that has stood by and watched their country fall has survived." With my wheels still turning, I say to myself, "I can't just stand by and watch my household fall financially, I gotta do something." What did I do? I got a second job, made a list of all of my expenses, added them up , and posted them on my fridge. I stood back, looked at my financial plan, and I declared right then and there, "I'm done with barely making it."

Throughout that whole month I went to work with a smile on my face knowing exactly how much my expenses, are and how much I need to make to pay them. No more negative accounts for me! I stuck with my financial plan and I had no more negative balances in my bank account, but I noticed every time I paid rent I would have a $0.00 balance. That made me extremely frustrated. I went home and thought to myself, "Where the crap is my money going?" "I don't understand. I know I have "x" amount of dollars a month in expenses, I make sure not to live above my means. Why am I not saving money?" Not too long ago I read this scripture in The Bible. It states, "His divine power has given us everything we need for life..." In other words God has given us everything we need to get out of the situation we are in. We only have to learn how to work it. That got my wheels turning again. So I went to work thinking, "How the crap do I use what He's given me? I'm an actor in Los Angeles and that's what I'm trying to do, use the talent He has given me." A little frustrated with my situation, I go to work. I am in a little cubbyhole talking to a co-worker of mine, her name is Lilo. It's around the end of the month or the beginning of a new one and she says to me, "I have no money." I'm thinking, "me either." For some reason those couple of sentences made something click. I thought of all the times I have been in that cubbyhole having that same conversation with other co-workers. I said to Lilo, "I wonder why servers are always broke. If you look at it we make a lot of money. We make $50 to $100 a shift plus a paycheck every two weeks that's around $20.00 or more an hour, if there's anybody that should NOT be broke it's us."

As I served my tables I thought back to when I was working for a news station back home, I was broke then too. While I was working there I did an interview with this banker and I was telling her I was trying to figure out how to make more money. Her response to me was, "If you can't learn how to manage a small amount of money, you'll never learn how to manage a large sum of it."

At the time I thought to myself, "You're just being dismissive." I was looking for a get rich quick plan, the Holy Grail. While serving, I thought about the scripture I mentioned, and what the banker told me, and I said, "Oh My Father in Heaven, I have to work with what I've got!" So I took another look at my financial plan and realized why my account was at zero every month. I found that I did the right thing by adding up my expenses , but I was matching my expenses with my income. Let's say my expenses are $2000 a month. The problem with me and most of my co-workers is that our goal was to make $2000 (or whatever our total expenses were) a month, which is why everyone was scrambling at the end of the month to make ends meet. If our expenses are $2000 and we are striving to save $2000, we are breaking even everytime we pay our bills for the month. This puts our accounts at zero dollars. Don't forget going out to bars and hanging with friends. That is what pushes the account into the negative.

Okay, I have found the problem. How do I fix it? How do we fix this problem? Hmph, "God has given us everything we need", and we have to learn how to manage what He has given us. This book will show how I've learned to do just that, manage a small amount of money, thus showing us how to manage a large sum of it. Let's do it together.

Income HIGHER than expenses

Well, you might have guessed it, but the first thing I learned is not to let my expenses match my income. That was the number one mistake I made, growing up as a teen as well. I would get a credit card or buy a new car thinking, "Okay, if I buy this new car add that with my insurance and my other expenses it'll total to be around, for example, $700 a month. Okay, okay, I make $750 a month. Let me see, that will leave me with $50 a month. Yes, I can get the car!" Um, no. I couldn't be more wrong because my expenses are almost matching my income. If something breaks down on that car that costs about $300 and I only have $50 for the month, I'm going to have a huge problem. I have to get $250 dollars from somewhere. So I have to make a choice: take it out of my car note to get it fixed, because I don't want to lose my insurance, or pay the car note and let the car sit in the garage. Hmm, if I don't have a car I can't go to work. I guess that rules that out. I guess it has to come out of the car note. Right there, ladies and gentlemen, is the beginning of America's debt. I have a negative hit on my credit report to this day because I leased a car that I could not afford. What's sad is I'm not the only one. Did you know 70% of Americans live check to check? That means only 30% of Americans are actually saving money for a rainy day, and the rest of us are a step away from living in poverty. Do you know we have the same problem even with our U.S. soldiers!? I know a guy working for a financial services company, one guy working at a restaurant, one guy in retail, and a few family members who are active and retired military men. All of which have talked about how the military gives these huge lump sums of cash when they completed basic training, and even larger sums of money if they got deployed. Another thing they told me was how much money they blew away buying material things, helping out their family, and so on. They also talk about how they would do things differently now that all the money is gone. After asking them, I discovered that these guys had one thing in common. They all had money problems before they joined the military. Heck, some of them joined the military so they could get rid of their money problems. I remember seeing this special on Oprah (yes I watch Oprah, shut up) where these guys did an experiment and gave this homeless man around one million dollars. He spent all of the money and ended up homeless all over again. That's when I realized the answer to being financially stable isn't always having more money, it's knowing how to manage it. Wow, I guess the banker was right. When I discovered this, I thought to myself, "Why wasn't I ever taught this. One problem is most Americans are not taught how to manage money at home or in school. If we are taught, it is some crazy accounting, debits, and credits class and it's not simplified. Since they didn't, I will. Here's a plan for us. The first step in *The Financial Plan for Tipmakers and everyday people* is to remember this formula: INCOME over EXPENSES. Always make sure your income at least doubles your expenses. For example, if you're expenses are $500 a month you should be making $1000 a month or more. If your income isn't two times more than your expenses it's okay, try to get it as close as you can. The first thing I did to try and get my expenses lower than my income is I cut back on unnecessary expenses. Some companies are going to be upset with me right now and for that I apologize. Here are some examples of trimming my expenses:

Gym membership: $60 a month.
I cancelled this because I can workout at home I was a martial artist for several years and I remember all of my exercises. It's also a good excuse to get back into it. If

you are one of those people who need to go to the gym, look for deals. One facility had a special for $20 a month. I don't know if it's still available, but it was a great deal. The catch is you could only go three times a week, depending on your workout routine, it's not a bad deal. Because of my decision to cancel my gym membership it allowed me to save $60 dollars a month. If I decided to simply reduce it to the $20 plan I can save $40, which is still good.

Cable: $60 a month.

I'm never home anyway. I Don't need it. Once again, you don't have to cancel and go cold turkey like I did. You can simply downgrade to a cheaper plan. Once again look for deals. Dish network had a special for around $20 a month. This reduction in cost is the same as the gym membership. Now I have just saved $120 a month.

Girlfriend: "Too much money a month.

"For those of who are in relationships or dating I joke about a plan I have called "Pimpin' on a budget." No, I'm not really a pimp, I just call it that. What I do is Google fun things to do in my city. A lot of the local news stations have a community events calendar which lists the things going on throughout the month. You'll be surprised at the things you can do for very cheap or for free! You can do things like having a picnic, going to an art class for a one time fee, rent movies, going to galleries. The cool thing is, is you can show your date a side of the city they have never seen before and you look like "The Man" or "The Wo-man" because you are always in the know. Guys I don't know about your lady, but mine loves to take trips, geez! So, I had to talk to her about my plan (more like negotiate). I said, "Babe, would you rather take a bunch of little trips once a month, or take one big trip once a year and really get to enjoy ourselves and not worry about having spending money?" I have to say she liked the idea of taking one big trip. She has something to look for all year, plus the trip will be better organized.

I think you get the idea. Look at your expenses and see where you can do some trimming. Don't try to be a hot shot and drive the nicest cars and wear the nicest clothes. I have a co-worker who is always complaining of being broke yet they are always taking trips out of town. Go figure. Be patient. The money will come. A friend of mine is the nephew of the actor Eriq La Salle. He told me for several years while Eriq was on the show E.R. he drove a basic car, something like a Honda Civic. He had a huge house, but a basic car. I'm sure Eriq could more than afford an expensive car, but owning a great home was more important and a great asset. Now my friend and I, being naïve, didn't mind driving, at least, a used model Mercedes while still living in an apartment. Eriq told this to my friend and I am passing it to you. He said, "Don't purchase a car when you can't afford the up keep." So my fellow co-workers and everyday people no matter how bad we want to be flashy, we have to be disciplined in our finances. With our feet firmly planted, otherwise we'll never reach our financial goals. Some people spend their whole lives working and have nothing to show for it, waiting to strike it rich, or waiting for a hand out. I don't know about you, but I don't like waiting on anyone to give me anything. Let's get it.

****
The Financial mind-set

Alright, I don't want you to have to read through a bunch of fluff just to get to the meat of this book. So I'm going to try to be brief as possible. People say it is better to have loved and lost than to not have loved at all, I believe money is different. I am very thankful I have not been blessed with a lot of money, yet then have it basically thrown into the garbage. Yes, I have made some financial mistakes, however it could have been worse. That is what I say to you as well, even if you have made lots of money and you have been knocked back to square one, which has happened to a lot of us right about now. It still could have been worse. I once heard a preacher say, " A set back is a set up for your comeback!" With that said Jesus explains perfectly what that banker told me about managing a small budget in one scripture.

He says, "No one sews a patch of unshrunk cloth on an old garment, for the patch will pull away from the garment, making the tear worse. Neither do men pour new wine into old wineskins. If they do, the skins will burst, the wine will run out and the wineskins will be ruined. No, they pour new wine into the new wineskins, and both are preserved." (Google this scripture if you want to know more)

That scripture wasn't about finances, but the same philosophy can be applied here. If we have an **old financial mind-set** and we are given **new** money, then we will be like the old wineskin and burst. In other words we will just end up losing it again. So don't be upset because your parents weren't rich or financially educated. Let's be the change in our homes and become like the new wineskin.

Controlling the uncontrollable

Now the meat... The reason it is so hard for waiters and other tip makers to save money is because tips are hard to keep track of. We really don't know how much we are going to make when we walk into the door. Some days can be really slow, we get sent home early, and go home with 20 bucks in our pocket. Other days can be super busy and we go home with like $200. There's nothing we can do about that. We can't control that. I heard Suze Orman say that we have to talk about our money and how much we make. So I'm going to be very real with you. This was my first financial plan with all of my expenses and real numbers. For the everyday people yours is a lot more simple, nonetheless, pay close attention. This is how I learned to control the uncontrollable.

-Calculate monthly expenses-

Monthly Obligations

$708.88 (rent)

$280.00 (child support)

$10.00 (greenpeace)

$100.00 (phone)

$104.00 (car insurance)

$90.00 (gasoline)*

$120.00 (groceries)*

$200.00 (bull)*

$40.00 (hair-cut)

total------$1652.88

Above is a list of all of my monthly obligations, the amount, and the total. Your list may differ from mine. Some may be more, some may be less. Don't be discouraged. I want you to note a couple of things. This is a list of my monthly obligations **after** I have cut back on my expenses like cable and etc. There is no particular reason for that. I just so happened to get the idea for this financial plan after I cut back. I urge you to make a list of your monthly obligations, first, that will allow you to see where you can cut back on your expenses. Some people I have shown this plan to have actually said my expenses are really low. To those people I want to let you know I have two jobs, and with those jobs combined I work a total of about 36 hours a week. That doesn't even equal ONE full time job. My server job is only 3days a week and I make only $7.50 an hour. My other restaurant job I only work 2days and I make $12.00 an hour. My expenses may seem low to some people, but my income is also low. If I can do it, so can you.

To explain a couple things about my "Monthly obligations" list, you may have noticed there are asterisks next to gasoline, groceries, and bull. "Bull" is a name I use for all the miscellaneous things I spend money on like going out to bars after work, movies, and etc. anything that is not a necessity. I placed an asterisk by the expenses that can easily get out of hand. For example: The times you have gone out and gotten a snack, fast food, or bought food on your lunch break. Those things don't have a set amount like rent or car insurance. What I have done is I have taken the items that don't have a set amount and have made them a monthly expense by giving them a limit, thus controlling the uncontrollable. I will explain in depth later. You may be wondering what percentage of your income you should use for rent and housing expenses, entertainment and etc. Many financial guides suggest using 1/3 of your net income (which means after taxes) for each. I use 32% of my net income for rent, 5.5% each for grocery and gas (some suggest 13%), and 9% of my net income for my bull list. As you begin to save more, I recommend speaking with a financial advisor and/or a wealth management company. After all, that is the point isn't it, to be wealthy? They will show you how to, even better, manage your finances and get you out of debt. They usually do taxes and investments as well. Talking to a personal banker at your local branch is a way to get *free* financial advice.

In the paragraph above I mentioned how much I make hourly (to the everyday people who may not know how a server's income works, server's make an hourly wage plus tips. At my $12 an hour job I do not make tips). What I'll do next is calculate the sum of my controllable income (hourly pay). See example below.

-Hourly income-

Job #1- $206.50 (every 2 weeks)
Job #2- $206.50 (every 2 weeks)

total----$413.00 (every 2weeks)
_____x2 (paid twice a month)

sum----$826.00 (every month)

In the chart above titled "Hourly income" you will see my pay cycle and how much I get paid. To be brief, I receive two checks twice a month, which brings the sum of my hourly income to $826.00. The next step will be to subtract my hourly income from my "monthly obligations." See example below:

-Expenses minus income-

$1,652.88 (monthly obligations)
- $826.00 (hourly income)

_$826.88 (remaining) = my "tip goal" or "financial obligations number"

The step shown above in the "Expenses minus income" chart is one of the most crucial steps. The reason is most servers can't wait until payday so they can cash that check and go shopping or get other necessities. Eeerh! Wrong! Do Not Cash That Check. Take it and put it into your account. Your paycheck should be a sign of relief. Noted in the "Expenses minus income" chart above, hourly, I make $826.00 a month. If I blow away a paycheck every time I get paid, that means, I have to make One Thousand Six Hundred Fifty Two Dollars and Eighty Eight Cents in Tips! That is way too much pressure. When I take my paychecks and deposit them into my account, that is $826.00 a month I don't have to worry about. As you can see my paychecks take a huge chunk out of my "monthly obligations," about half to be exact. Someone may ask the question, "What about spending money?" It's already included in my "Monthly obligations" chart.

It is my miscellaneous category, which I affectionately call my "bull" list. My bull is my spending money.

"Everyday people," you do not have to worry about making tips. Your portion of the "Financial Plan…" is almost complete, however there is one major part of the plan missing. Stay tuned… Also to those who are trying to get their income higher than expenses, get another job, but do not take on another expense after you get that job. That only raises your expenses again and puts you back where you started. Not everyone has the will power to do it, but that's difference between the rich and poor.

Now this is the point where I mentioned earlier when I had gone to work super excited waiting to try out my new financial plan. I later realized my financial plan at this point was not complete. Note the "Expenses minus income" chart above. I saw that I had $826.88 remaining after deducting my "hourly income." This means to me and many other servers around the world that all I had to do was make $826.88 a month in tips. Which in Los Angeles, is very achievable. That was a mistake because when I paid my rent my account went right back to zero. This is where I got frustrated. It's funny when I think about it, because after all of that calculating I somehow made my expenses match my income. I realized if after deducting paycheck my new "monthly obligation" is $826.88 and I make my "tip goal" $826.88, forgive me for sounding redundant, but $826.88 minus $826.88 equals ZERO! I discovered I needed a smaller goal. I'll explain:

While serving at a restaurant I met the writer Antwone Fisher a few years ago. He gave me this advice, "Writing is like chopping down a tree, you cut it down one swipe at a time." I took that advice and applied it to my financial plan. I asked myself the question, "I wonder if I could achieve my "tip goal" of $826.88 at the beginning of the month by chopping a piece of my monthly obligations each day I served tables?" This is where I realized my financial plan needs another step. I got out my pen and pad and did the math. Okay, I serve 3 shifts a week and there are 4 weeks in a month. 3 x 4= 12, which means I serve 12 shifts a month. See tip goal divided by shifts chart below:

-Tip goal divided by shifts-

$826.88 (tip goal)

_____/12 (3 shifts x 4 weeks a month)

$68.91 (each shift!) my "daily tip goal"

Observe "tip goal divided by shifts" chart above. You will notice that darn number again $826.88. By now it's probably ringing in your ears. That's good! I believe everyone should know their "financial obligations number." I wake up out of my sleep and scream $826.88! I don't mean that literally, by the way. Knowing my "financial obligations number" empowers me because I know my limits. Knowing my limits allows me to judge whether or not I can take on a new expense and live comfortably, or if I have to cut out something in order to save money and live comfortably. Once you finish reading and replace my financial obligations list with your own personal numbers your "financial obligations number" will be ringing in your ears instead of mine. Note the "tip goal divided by shifts" chart again. When I divided my "tip goal" by the number of shifts I work a month I now have a new number. My new number is the "daily tip goal." My daily tip goal is $68.91! I mentioned earlier that a lot of servers make around 100 dollars a shift or more right? Okay servers and tip makers, how easy is it for you to make sixty eight dollars and ninety one cents a day!? Check this out, all expenses are paid! Note the financial obligations chart (if you need to). With just $68.91 a day I have just taken care of my groceries, rent, my son, haircut, spending money, and etc. After doing the math for the "tip goal divided by shifts" chart I thought to myself, "Oh my Father in Heaven, how much money have I been spending!?" Someone may ask, "What about the days when tips are low or business is slow?" Because business these days is kind of hit or miss, this is what I do now. I said I work 3 shifts a week right? So I just multiply my daily tip goal by 3shifts or in your case however many shifts you work a week. See "weekly tip goal" chart below.

-Weekly tip goal-

$68.91 (daily tip goal)

x_____3 (shifts a week)

$206.73 (or $207.00 a week)

Note the "weekly tip goal" chart above. As you can see my weekly tip goal is $207.00. It's like I said before, servers make around $100.00 or more a shift, $207.00 a week is very attainable. Tip makers, you know sometimes we can make $207 in a day! I'll say again, I save $207.00 every week and all of my bills are paid including spending money. Just a heads up, it is important to keep track of how much you make in tips daily by making a chart of your work week write the day, the date, and how much you made. This way you know if you are reaching your weekly goal. For example: On Monday, I might have gone home with $40.00 in tips and the other two days I went home with $150. I didn't reach my goal on Monday, but at the end of the week I made $340.00. My goal was still achieved, yet notice what has happened. My "weekly tip goal" is only $207.00, but I made $340.00 for the week. I now have $133.00 that I can put into my savings. I have already set a cap for my spending money, which is $200.00. Why do I need to spend $133.00 more? I don't. Remember the spending money is included in the weekly tip goal. Once you have reached it, whatever is left over can go into your savings account.

Wow! I hope you are excited as I was when I first created this financial plan. I am still excited to see how much money I can save and feeling like I can actually control my money. However, we are not out of the woods yet. Note the "monthly obligations" chart. Do you remember the things I put asterisks by? Do you remember when I said I'll explain in depth later? The items with asterisks are the items on my list that I can easily lose control of: Gas, Grocery, and Bull. To reiterate, it's easy to drive more this week than you did last week ("gas"). Maybe you are having some friends over and you want to cook dinner ("grocery"). What if those friends want to come over to eat every Sunday and watch football? Hey, Jenni. What if there are a few movies out that you want to see ("bull")? You're going to need movie snacks ("bull"). The co-workers want to go to the local bar after work (more "bull"). What I have done is I have taken the items with asterisks and created a chart which allows me to keep track of those items that can get out of hand. This chart is called the "Uncontrollable Items Chart." These are real numbers from my actual uncontrollable items chart for one month.

(see next page)

-Uncontrollable items-chart-

AUGUST: deadline for expenses/9-1-09

T I P S / E X P E N S E S

TIPS	GAS- $80.00	GROCERY-$120.00	BULL-$200.00
week 1:			
sat. 8/8/09	$12.00	$6.00 icecream	$40.00 herbs
$100.00	$10.00	$3.00 dvd	$68.00
	$20.00	$7.00 lunch @ work	$3.00 internet use
week 2:	$20.00	$12.10 grocery	$22.00 music store
mon.8/10/09	$20.05	$3.00 misc	$10.00 post office
$59.00	$18.00	$11.30 grocery	$26.00 movies
tue.8/11/09		$3.29 cereal	$5.00 carwash
$170.00		$28.24 grocery	$8.00 game rental
sat.8/15/09		$4.00 junkfood	$10.00 game controller
$120.00		$5.00 face products	$2.00 parking
		$3.10 misc	$44.00 movies
week 3:		$12.50 grocery	$9.00 beer
mon.8/17/09		$3.59 junkfood	$5.00 junkfood
$74.00		$13.00 grocery	$6.28 grocery
tue.8/18/09			
$120.00		total: $118.12	total: $193.28
sat.8/22/09		balance: $1.88	balance: $6.72
$120.00			
week 4:			
mon.8/24/09	**learned***	**learned***	
$87.00	week 1: $20.00	week 1: $50.00	
tue.8/25/09	week 2: $90.00	week 2: $50.00	
$69.00	week 3: $20.00	and etc.	
thu.8/27/09	week4: $20.00		
$140.00	and etc.		
mon/8/31/09			
$49.00			
total: $1108.00!!!			
savings: $276.07			

R E M A I N I N G

GAS		GROCERY		BULL	
8/6/2009	$68.00	8/6/2009	$108.00	8/6/2009	$132.00
8/8/2009	$56.00	8/7/2009	$101.00	8/13/2009	$96.00
8/12/2009	$38.00	8/8/2009	$97.90	8/17/2009	$71.00
8/18/2009	$17.95	8/8/2009	$94.90	8/20/2009	$66.00
8/25/2009	-0.05	8/9/2009	$80.31	8/26/2009	$13.00
		8/10/2009	$80.31	8/27/2009	$6.72
		8/13/2009	$80.31	8/31/2009	-.5
		8/17/2009	$48.07		
		8/17/2009	$28.53		
		8/18/2009	$24.96		
		8/19/2009	$11.96		
		8/31/2009	$0.00		

Fyi, this chart comes in handy when trying to apply for an apartment. As a server, the apt. manager will ask how much do you make in tips. You can prove your hourly wage with your paystubs. How do you prove your tips? You can prove it with this chart by calculating exactly how much you make a month by keeping track of your daily tip goal. If I were an apartment manager I would be very impressed to see how you kept track of your tips. If they see you are that serious about your money they will be more willing to lend to you. With that said, don't throw away your charts.

On the "Uncontrollable items- chart" for August you will see my deadline is 9-1-09. The first of the month is my new favorite date. You may ask, "What if my bills are due on the 15th?" When I made this plan I did not pay utilities. I have since moved into a better apartment. I now pay utilities. This may sound oversimplified, but I simply pay my bills when they are due. It has already been calculated into my budget when I totaled all of my expenses. If the funds are not available in your checking account because you are waiting on a paycheck or tips, it's okay to transfer money from your savings. A lot of financial advisors advise against transferring money from your savings. If you have to do this, be cautious. This can be very tempting for some people to keep the extra money instead of replacing it. Remember to always, **always** replace the money you borrowed from your checking once you have received your new paycheck.

Note the "Uncontrollable Items Chart." Just as I mentioned in the preceding paragraphs I have taken the items with an asterisk from my "monthly obligations list" and categorized them. I have organized them into two columns one labeled "expenses" and the other labeled "remaining." I will guide you through the chart by following the "gas" expense (this one is easier to follow). As I have written, I have set a cap for my "gas" expense in the amount of $80.00. Be advised, this was written before prices for gas reached over $4.00 a gallon. I was also driving a much smaller vehicle then. The gas I am speaking of is gasoline, not the utility. Look at the chart under the "expenses" side and you will see on my first trip to the gas station I spent $12.00. Now refer to the "remaining" side of the chart. I have put the date 8/6/2009 and the dollar amount of $68.00. This amount is how much I have left for the rest of the month to spend on gas ($80.00 - $12.00= $68.00). To elaborate: whenever I spend money on gas, grocery, or bull I make a note of what it is, how much it cost, and deduct it from my monthly allowance in the grocery, gas, or bull column under the "expenses" category. After I deduct the item from my monthly allowance what is left over goes in the "remains" category, so I'll know how much I can spend for the rest of the month. F.Y.I. the reason I thought the "gas" expense would be easier to follow rather than the other expenses is because the dates in the other columns are not congruent to the items I purchased. For example: In the "expenses" category under "bull" I have fourteen purchased items, but in the "remaining" category I only have seven dates. The reason for that is some days I was in a rush or whatever the excuse was, and some of my receipts accumulated for a day or two before I did the math on the dates listed. Since then I have learned it is extremely important to make note of the money you spend daily. The reason is you can easily lose track or go over budget.

Creating and following this particular month's uncontrollable items chart was the most difficult part of the financial plan for me, which is why I chose to use it as an example. It was difficult because this chart changed how I looked at my finances by showing me what I spend my money on. I learned that I spend a lot of my money on junk food. It also changed how I managed my money from month to month. It doesn't sound that difficult I know, but a lot of times change is uncomfortable. Then and even now when I look at this chart it tells me a lot about myself. Note the <u>expenses category</u>: notice at the top of the month I spent $12.00 on gas. Which was August 6th, but two days later on the 8th I spent 10 more dollars on gas. I don't know what type of car you have, but twelve dollars doesn't fill up my tank. Even though this plan worked on paper, I didn't quite trust it yet. Because of the recent times I rarely filled my tank all the way until I created this plan. I wound up going to the gas station five times in the month of August because I feared I would run out of money, not because I drove a lot. Nonetheless, gas wasn't the only expense I was fearful of paying in its entirety. My phone bill was another one, even though it's not on the uncontrollable items chart. I know you don't do this (sarcasm), but I used to pay only half of a bill so I can have money for a rainy day. This is also how you can get behind in your expenses and get into debt. By personalizing this chart to your needs you will know how much money you are spending and how much you have to work with. Hopefully it won't take you a month like me, but once you have created your chart and cut out unnecessary expenses stick to it. Trust the math. It's like Jay-Z said, "People lie, numbers don't."

Observe the "<u>Uncontrollable Items Chart</u>," look under the column entitled "tips." As you can see I have kept track of how much I made in tips each day. I serve only three days a week minimum and every week except the first week I have made over my "weekly tip goal." 3 days a week is what I use to calculate my income because I have three guaranteed shifts. It's what I have on schedule. If I usually pick up 2 days a week it would not be safe to use 5 days to calculate my income b/c those days are not guaranteed. After all of my expenses were paid, I was very excited to see that I had overflow. As listed under my monthly obligations I only need to make $826.88 in tips a month. Much to my delight I have made $1108.00, which means I have saved $281.12. This chart made me think, "If ended up having a zero balance at the end of the month, how much money had I been wasting? I used to make more money than this before the recession." There's a few things about the chart I did not tell you. First, I'll state the obvious. You'll notice I highlighted grocery in the amount of $6.28 under the "bull" column. The reason for that is because I have maxed out in the grocery column and I saw I had a few more dollars left in my spending money so I used it to buy groceries. This will happen from time to time some months you'll spend more in one column than the other. That's why I call this the uncontrollable items chart. Now, for the not so obvious: on the chart under the "expenses" category in each column you see the word "learned." This is what I learned from my September chart, which is not included in this book. In the month of September I was so excited because of the money I saved in August, I had true faith in my numbers. So, I went and bought a bunch of groceries, and a bunch of bull, and two weeks into the month I started nearing my limit and I was once again asking this question, "Where did my money go?" I am glad I learned this so you won't make the same mistake. To explain what the "learned" columns mean: take all of your monthly allowances and divide them by four because there are four weeks in a month. For example, my monthly allowance for groceries is $120.00, therefore I can only spend $30.00 a week, or $60.00 every two weeks. Once again, don't be intimidated if my numbers are smaller than yours. By dividing your monthly allowance weekly or bi-weekly it allows you to allocate your funds throughout the month.

Another thing that I did not tell you is. In the "tips" column I actually made more than what is listed. I made 10% more to be exact. Before I get home and write down how much I made for the day in tips I take out 10% for my tithes to give to God (for those who don't know "tithes" is when you put your money in the basket at church). I don't even write it down on my uncontrollable items chart because the tithe doesn't belong to me anyway. The tithe belongs to God (Google the scripture). I used to be so afraid to pay the full tithe because I would count how much I had taken out throughout the week and see how much money I could have if I didn't take out that freakin' tithe. I know it's not right to say, but it's real. Then God said to trust Him. He said if I give my tithe He'll not only protect the rest of my money, but He'll bless me so much that I will not have room for it (Malachi 3:10-12). God also says, "Test me in this." Are you kidding me? God is giving me permission to test him. What do I have to lose? Ten percent is only a dime. If I have a dollar God wants a dime?! So I give my tithes and now I have overflow. My cup is not flooding over so much that I can't handle yet, but it is overflowing. Didn't mean to give you a Bible lesson there, but I said I was going to give you the real numbers from my "Uncontrollable Items Chart." Giving my tithes to God is part of my finances.

****
Everyday People

Okay, now for the everyday people. I didn't have you sit through that whole thing for nothing. Thanks for hanging in there. F.Y.I. your financial plan it will be a lot simpler. Servers, I want you to read this section as well. You won't be making tips your whole lives unless your career goal is to be a server. The financial plan for everyday people is for set incomes based on hourly wage and/or salary. Everyday people, you will still have to follow a lot of the same steps in your financial plan as the servers with just some slight differences. Here goes: Your "Uncontrollable items chart" is the same except you don't have to worry about keeping track of your tips so you may omit the "tips" column. Just like the servers you will still need to create a list of your monthly obligations and calculate the total (as seen below).

-E.P. plan (everyday people plan)-

Monthly Obligations

$708.88 (rent)

$280.00 (child support)

$10.00 (greenpeace)

$100.00 (phone)

$104.00 (car insurance)

$90.00 (gasoline)*

$120.00 (groceries)*

$200.00 (bull)*

$40.00 (hair-cut)

total------$1652.88

Next: you will need to calculate how much you make a month then subtract your monthly obligations from your income. Below, is my monthly income converted if I made an hourly wage only.

-E.P. plan Income minus Expenses-

$1,934.00 (Monthly Income)

-$1,652.88 (Monthly obligations or expenses)

= $281.12 (savings)

I went over $5.05 in my "uncontrollable" spending which leaves me with a savings of $276.07

Note: the "E.P. plan Income minus Expenses" chart above. Notice I said I spent $5.05 over my plan. This is why it is important to keep track in your "uncontrollable items" chart daily and not to let your receipts accumulate. By the time you realize you have gone over your limit it may be too late. Thank God I only went over $5.05.

To reiterate, when you subtract your expenses from your income and the difference equals savings is because your spending money is included in your monthly obligations list. Treat your spending money as an expense. Warning: the E.P. plan at this point has the same flaw as the server's plan. When you subtract your monthly obligations from your monthly income it puts your expenses goal at the end of the month and causes you to have to scramble at the end of the month to pay your bills, thus causing you to live paycheck to paycheck. Instead take your monthly income and divide it by two or by four, depending on if you get paid weekly or bi-weekly. See below:

$1,934 (monthly income)
____/2 (bi-weekly)
= $967 (income every two weeks)

Then take the sum of your monthly obligations and divide it by two or by four as well. See below:

$1,562.88 (expenses)

_____/2 (bi-weekly)

= $781.44 (this amount goes to expenses every paycheck)

I feel like some of you are getting scared. I have to say again... *Your spending money is included in the $781.44* do not worry. Hey, look at what happened. If you make $967 (bi-weekly), and your expenses are $781.44 (bi-weekly), then you are saving a minimum of $185.56 every two weeks. I say minimum because you may not spend all of your "bull" money and what is left at the end of the month goes right into your savings! When you divide your monthly obligations it will allow you to knock off some of your expenses each week or every other week throughout the month. Nevertheless, some expenses can be tricky. I was showing this plan to a relative who was having financial trouble. She told me that her expenses exceeded her income and once a year she had to pay taxes on her house. She said each year it was a struggle because she only gets paid salary once a month. I told her first, she has to cut back on expenses. Then I asked her how much did she pay for the taxes. I don't remember the exact number, but she said something like $500.00. So I thought for a second about Antwone Fisher's ten minute rule and I told her since she gets paid once a month, and taxes are due once a year, there are twelve months in a year, so chop down that $500 one check at a time. $500 divided by 12= $41.67 or $42.00 a month. She was excited to see instead of scrambling for what seemed to be the impossible amount of $500.00 at the end of the year all she had to do was save $42.00 a month. To the homeowners I hope that story helped you a little. If you own a home divide your annual expenses by 12 (months a year) or by 52 (weeks a year) and make them a monthly expense. Just look, If you get paid every other week: $500 divided 26 (every two weeks for one year) =

$19.53. Yes, if you're paying $500 a month for property taxes you can pay it off by at this rate by saving $20.00 every paycheck. By the way if you have an unexpected expense, for example, an oil change simply add it to your monthly obligations list for that month. If your oil change is $45.00 add $45.00 to the sum of your monthly obligations list. Rule of thumb: when possible breakdown your expenses as much as you can before the due date. It is better to save up for an expense in small increments than to try to pay it in full on the due date.

The same principle can apply to your savings account. Even though, with this financial plan you don't have to set aside money to save, but if you want you should try this: Before I created the *"The Financial Plan for Tipmakers..."* I created another way to save money. I noticed I used to buy lunch almost every time I went to work and on my off days I realized I would spend more than that. So I told myself, "I know I spend at least five dollars a day. Why don't I try to save that?" So a savings plan was born. I thought, "The average person works five days a week and is off two." So I decided to save five dollars every week for five days. If I waited tables that day I would take five dollars and put it into the bank. If I worked my hourly job, I would transfer five dollars from my checking account to my savings account. If I was supposed to work and decided to take the day off I would still save five dollars. I did the math and discovered $5.00 x 5 days a week =$25. There are 52 weeks in a year so, $25 x 52 weeks = $1300. Wow! I know the average person spends waay more than five dollars a day. If you can afford to save five dollars in addition to your financial plan, I strongly recommend it. I stopped the five dollars a day savings plan because I kept withdrawing from my savings account. It seemed every time I saved about a hundred or so I had to pinch from it. Like I said, I thought of the five dollar savings before I created *"The Financial*

Plan for Tipmakers..." That means I didn't have an "Uncontrollable Items Chart." In other words I didn't know how to manage my money properly.

I currently am not using the five dollar savings because it's not within my financial means, and that's okay. With the new plan, I save around $200.00 a month which is actually double the amount I would save with the five dollar savings plan. I am happy that I can say it's not within my financial means because that's what this plan is about. *The Financial Plan for Tipmakers and Everyday People* allows us to know our financial strengths and weaknesses. A great warrior knows all of his strengths and all of his weaknesses. The good thing about a great warrior is he will work on those weaknesses until they become his/ her strengths. I initially created this financial plan for myself because I had a lot of financial weaknesses. When I shared this plan with my friends I noticed we became aware of our finances. We got stronger financially and are getting even stronger. I heard Barack Obama say while he was running for office, "The way to rebuild this economy is from the bottom up." When you think about it, it's the lower and middle class that make up most of America. It's the lower and middle class that are losing the most jobs. It's the lower and middle class that have to cut waay back on household spending and it is the lower and middle class that are the consumers. Servers, barbers, tipmakers, and everyday people, we are the lower and middle class, we are the "bottom"...Let's start building.

-Cornelious Jordan

The good book says, "Meekness is power under control." Therefore, I say meekness is a writer, actor, or director scrubbing floors. It's the image of a Lamborghini driving in the slow lane. YOU have the power!

Thank you for reading.

######

Now you have finished the book, give it a try for yourself. Create your own uncontrollable items chart! The far left column is intended to for tips, but you may use that column however you like. Control the uncontrollable!

All the best,

Cornelious Jordan

www.ingramcontent.com/pod-product-compliance
Lightning Source LLC
Chambersburg PA
CBHW071550170526
45166CB00004B/1615

* 9 7 8 1 4 9 0 4 2 1 6 2 9 *